Blogging for Beginners

By

Khalid Zidan

SuccessEntrepreneur.org

Table of Contents

Getting Started

Imagine a job where you could get paid to share your opinions about things that you're passionate about—a job that you can do from your own home with totally flexible hours that takes almost nothing in the way of upfront financial investment.

For many people, that job is blogging. It's no wonder that close to 1% of American adults make at least a portion of their living by blogging. The Bureau of Labor Statistics reports that about 2 million people profit from blogging each year in America. Of those, about a quarter (452,000 people) use blogging as their primary source of income.

If you want to become a successful blogger, this information is both uplifting and depressing. It is possible to make money blogging; lots of people are already doing it. But like with other creative professions like actors and musicians, the people who don't make enough to quit their day job far outnumber famous celebrities earning millions of dollars. I won't lie and say it's easy making your living as a blogger, but it is true that anyone can do it, provided you have a subject you're passionate about and the dedication to write about it long-term.

Each chapter in this book explores a different element of blogging, from setting up your domain name to diversifying your income streams. Each chapter ends with wisdom from a person who started from nothing and found success through blogging. But while blogging is a possible profit opportunity for anyone, let's first clear up some popular misconceptions about blogging.

What Blogging is Not

A New Idea

Let's face it—it's 2016, and it seems like everybody has a blog. The ground floor gold rush of the early 2000s is over. You can use this to your advantage. Spend some time in the blogosphere before you start making your blog. Look at some successful blogs to see what they do right, but also, check out some unsuccessful blogs and figure out what they're doing wrong. Most importantly, look up other blogs on your chosen topic.

How saturated is your market? If it's a popular topic, that means there's a lot of interest and more potential customers, but it also means you'll have to compete against other more established brands. What value will your blog add to this area—and how will it stand out from the rest? Blogging has transitioned from an experimental concept to an established business model, and understanding this will help you to navigate the market more successfully from the outset.

A free-for-all

Again, the Wild West atmosphere of internet commerce in the early 2000s is gone. There are rules that you need to follow to stay a part of the blogging community. Some of these unspoken points of courtesy in how you treat the community, others are on the books rules that you could get sued or shut down for breaking.

Intellectual property rules are especially important to understand if you want to add images or media to your site. It might not be the exciting part of blogging, but knowing the rules up front will keep you from making costly mistakes.

A hobby

Well, it can be, in the same way playing guitar can be a hobby—and that's a big difference between your college roommate and Eric Clapton: one does it for fun, the other does it for a living. If you want to make money blogging, you have to look at it as a business. You can still have fun doing it, but you have to be willing to commit to it even when it's not fun if you want to make it work for you long-term.

Consistently providing high-quality content will mean dedicating time and effort to your blog. You should be prepared to commit at least 10 hours a week to your blog and to continue doing so even after the initial excitement has worn off.

An instant payoff

You'll hear about overnight successes in the blogging world, but what that most often means is that everybody on the internet realized the blog was there overnight. Most likely, that blogger has been going strong, writing content and working on building an audience, for years. For some of that time, the blogger was probably making little to no money.

Undoubtedly, they experienced some setbacks, and tried some things that didn't work, but they used those failures as learning experiences to improve and grow their business. The actual moment blogs are "discovered" by the big leagues might often be dictated by luck, but those lucky moments only come around after you've worked hard to make a quality product.

A stand-alone business

There are some bloggers who earn plenty from ad revenue alone, but many bloggers owe their financial success to a diversification of income streams. The most common way for bloggers to branch out is by making a product for their regular readers to buy, or by selling services related to their area of expertise.

If you don't want to make original products, affiliation with brands that do sell products can increase your earnings (Amazon's affiliate program is the best-known). Writing and selling eBooks has become an increasingly profitable extra income stream as self-publishing services have become more affordable and easier to use. Don't box yourself in by thinking of yourself only as a blogger and you'll open up a whole new world of potential profit opportunities.

Chapter 1: Finding your niche

You probably have some friends with personal blogs that are smorgasbords of all their interests—pictures of their kids and movie reviews and talk about their favorite sports team, and everything in between. While this is fine for a personal blog, if you want to blog professionally you should narrow your focus.

A blog that has a clear identity is more likely to be successful than one with a broad focus. A personal blog is about you while a professional blog is about the topic. You can and should be personable and share your story, but only as it relates to the topic at hand.

Before you start doing anything else to start your blog, you should figure out your topic. Your niche will impact the domain name you choose, the design of your page, and your ideal posting schedule to appeal to the most readers in your area.

Research the market

Picking the right market for a new blog can be tricky. You want to find a topic that is popular enough to attract interest and earn money, but one that hasn't already been oversaturated with bloggers giving their opinions.

Finding a new perspective on a topic, something that people aren't already blogging about, gives you the best chance of making it in the business long-term—if it's a field where interest exists, and the reason there are no bloggers on the topic isn't because no one wants to read about it. The only way to know is by researching the field.

The larger the interest in a given topic, the smaller percentage of the total market share you need to capture to be successful, and the more specialized your niche will be to provide a new voice. Let's use a food blog as an example. Food is a topic that interests a broad range of people—the overall potential readership is massive, but there are an accordingly high number of blogs already talking about food. Even if you narrow it down—say, to a blog about cooking—you'll already find thousands of other blogs already doing that.

The interest in the area is so high you'll need to narrow it down again. Maybe you're a vegan and want to share recipes for making traditional comfort food that's vegan-friendly. You'll probably find there are quite a few vegan bloggers out there, but the comfort food angle will make you just different enough to be a new voice in the conversation, and there are enough people interested in the topic that all of you can share the readership and be successful.

Now let's say you have a less popular topic—we'll use musical instrument repair as an example. Instrument repair is a practical subject that lots of people will be interested in, from professional musicians to band directors to people who play instruments for fun, but it won't encompass quite so broad a group as cooking.

You might do the research and find there are a lot of musical instrument review blogs, but not as many that focus on repair. Not only do you not need to break your topic down further into "wind instrument repair" or "on the fly repairs for rock musicians" but focusing on more will probably narrow your topic too much.

There isn't as much competition for instrument repair blogs as there is for food blogs, but the group of interested readers is also smaller, meaning you need to attract a larger percentage of interested readers to be successful.

Another way to think about this is to have a target audience size in mind numerically. Let's say you want to reach 1,000 unique subscribers. On the surface, the larger audience seems to give you the best statistical chance of being able to find more readers. If there are 100,000 people interested in X and only 10,000 interested in Y, that might seem to give you 10 times as many opportunities to make an impression on a unique reader.

But if 1,000 people are already blogging about X and only ten are blogging about Y that means the smaller group will nonetheless have more available readers per blogger. With X, you'd have to fight other bloggers to take away some share of their readership if you want to reach your goal; with Y, you could theoretically reach your target readership without having to share readers with any other blogger. The market may be smaller, but it's also less saturated.

Of course, things rarely work out that cleanly in the real world, but the ultimate point remains. The best niche for a new blog in 2016 isn't necessarily the one with the biggest following or the one that's the most unique; the best niche is the one that allows you to be a new voice for a community that will be able to support you.

You shouldn't assume what kind of activity exists on a given blog topic before you start doing your research. Some topics might seem like they'd be immensely popular but turn out to be relatively rare once you've done your research, making them perfect potential niches for you.

Conversely, you might think you're the only one interested in a given idea, only to find the blogosphere already overrun with people scribbling on your esoteric niche. Take notes as you do your research to kill two birds with one stone.

Bookmark blogs you like, either because of their look or the writing style of the author, then study those for ideas once your site is set up. If the blogs are in your niche, sign up for their mailing list, pay attention to their posts, and consider commenting and become part of their community once you've got your blog set up. It's never too early to start building goodwill (and good habits) in your blogging career.

Why you?

The blog itself is not the product you're selling to the consumer. The blog page is more like the storefront. The products that are up for sale are your ideas and expertise, as conveyed through your posts. To attract readers to your blog, you need to give them a reason to listen to what you, specifically, have to say about a given topic. Why would someone want to read your blog instead of the ones already established?

For an example, let's use the topic of professional baseball. There's a huge target audience, but what value do you have to offer to readers? Do you have an inside connection to the players? A new method of analysis for the games? Talking about how much you like something might be fun for you, but it's not very interesting to read.

The best bloggers have either a high level of expertise about their topic or bring a unique perspective to the table. Even if a given niche has a large potential audience and not many competing voices, you won't attract any readers if you don't have anything interesting to say about the topic. Before you make your final decision on which niche to delve into, ask yourself that simple question: why me? You should be able to provide a one-sentence answer that would make someone interested in reading what you have to say.

Logistics

If your blog fits naturally into your daily schedule and lifestyle, it'll be easier for you to put in the effort of maintaining it, and you'll be less likely to feel overwhelmed or give up due to burn-out. Make sure that the research, writing, and marketing you'll need to do in your chosen niche is realistic for your life before you settle on a topic. If you want to write about the local music scene, you'll have to make a point of going to a lot of shows— maybe not the best idea if you have to wake up early every day for work.

If you want to write a financial blog, you need to be able to keep up with market trends and deliver timely advice to your readers who are counting on you to guide them through a quickly changing landscape.

The niche you choose will also have an impact on how you earn profit from your blog. If you're writing in a larger niche, your ratio of fly-by traffic to repeat readers might be higher. You'll get a lot of page views that would appeal to advertisers, but may have a harder time selling products.

Conversely, a blog in a small niche that has a loyal core of followers might not get as much traffic, but the per-visitor profit could be higher because those visitors buy products and services, whether they're original to you or sold by an affiliate.

Blogging success story: Joe Gilder

Joe Gilder is the owner of HomeStudioCorner.com, a blog aimed at helping people set up home recording studios. Within six months of starting his blog, he had 500 subscribers on his e-mail list. By the time he sat down with Yaro Starak for his EJ Insider Interviews Club series, Gilder was on track to make $300,000 a year, with 13 different income streams all working for him through his blog.

Gilder is an example of someone who's found success by focusing in on a relatively small niche. He doesn't have as many readers as the best-known "celebrity" blogs, but the readers he does have are more loyal. More of his income is from his product range than it is from the traditional blog revenue sources, like advertising and affiliate programs.

He can continue to make a living through his blog even though he has less traffic than larger sites because he makes more per visitor, offering high-quality products that his readers benefit from buying.

Chapter 2: Domains and hosting

It can be tempting when you first start your blog to put it on a free site. After all, it's still a blog available on the internet, so why pay more than you have to set up? Free blog services are fine if you're a hobbyist, but they have major disadvantages that can make your life much harder as a professional blogger.

Free sites, in general, don't rank as well in search engines as paid domain names. They also don't give you as much control over your design, making the page look unoriginal and less professional. Some free services also run their own ads on your website, limiting your chances of making ad income.

Domain names

A domain name is your address on the internet (the part of the site that goes between "www" and ".com"). A new domain name can be claimed through a variety of different online services. A domain that has been registered may not be off limits; some people will buy domains to re-sell them though these are often far more expensive options.

It's not expensive to register a new domain name—doing it with GoDaddy can cost you as little as $10 a year, and other services offer domain registration in the $20 to $40 range. Some domain names are more expensive than others.

For a while when the first internet business boom was happening, investors would buy domain names with the intent of reselling them at a higher price, with some going for thousands or even millions of dollars (sex.com sold for $13 million in 2010, the current record; investing.com sold for $2.5 million in 2012). The bubble on this industry has burst, however, and even the most in-demand domains have seen their prices fall back down to earth.

If possible, your domain name should match the name of your blog. It doesn't have to; once you own your domain name, you can put whatever you want on that site. Matching the web address to the blog name, though, will give you more name and brand recognition and make it easier for readers to find you.

Think of some words and phrases related to your niche and your perspective on it. Once you've found a combination that you like, check if it's available through an online registration service. Generally speaking, single-word titles (especially those related to popular fields) are more likely to have been purchased by a domain investor and to cost extra money to obtain.

Let's use the example of the vegan comfort food cooking blog from chapter 1. Cooking and vegan are common words that are likely to be already used or, at least, to have been purchased by an investor. Think about the next level of your niche, then— the comfort food angle—and brainstorm possible combinations.

Two and three word combinations are less likely to have been used already. With a little creativity, you can find an open domain name that relates to your niche and is more quirky and memorable than "VeganCooking.com."

Hosting

Once your blog has a domain name it has an address, but it doesn't yet have a home. The files associated with your site will need to be hosted on a server so that your viewers can access them. There are many hosting sites out there. Many places that register domains also offer hosting services, which is convenient, though you should make sure the site has the services you need before signing up. Blue Host is a common hosting site for WordPress bloggers who are transitioning to a self-sufficient site.

The most important thing to consider is how much web traffic volume you can have on a particular hosting site. Bandwidth limits won't matter when you're first starting your blog, but if you hope to grow your traffic quickly, you shouldn't set yourself up for failure by choosing a server that's too small. A lot of hosting sites offer different tiers of packages at different rates depending on your traffic needs and make it easy to upgrade down the line.

You can typically pay for hosting month by month and while you usually get a bit of a discount for buying more time at once, paying monthly can let you try a service out if you're not sure whether or not it will work for you. Moving hosts can be a hassle but isn't as costly or difficult as changing domains would be; you can change your mind in the future without affecting your reader's ability to access your pages.

When you're first starting out, the cheapest option is often a shared hosting account. Prices can start as low as $1-$2 per month. Sites that offer this option include iPage, eHost, and In Motion Hosting. Research the hosting site before you sign up. Are they reliable, or do you see users complaining about their service? You can also check around with other bloggers and see what hosting sites they use.

Site builders and CMS

You've got a domain name and a host where the files associated with it can live. Now all you have to do is make your blog and transfer it to the host—and if you're not a technically-minded person, this can be very intimidating.

The level of involvement you want to have with the creation of the page code on your site will determine which kind of site editor or site builder is best for you. People use these terms in different ways, adding to the confusion.

A web editor gives you the most control over your page's design, but also requires some knowledge of HTML and CSS, and probably also things like JavaScript, PHP, and Perl for the kind of components most people want on a blog. The most basic web editor is a plain text program like Notepad. Plain text programs will require you to write all the code, but are the cheapest and most straightforward option.

Web editor programs like Dreamweaver and KompoZer have a visual interface for the user, making the website building experience more similar to designing a Word document than to writing computer code.

Once you've designed your pages with a web editor, you still need to get them onto your host's server using an FTP (File Transfer Protocol) program. Both the FTP program and the web editor will need to be installed on your computer, and you have full control over their use—the primary advantage of using this method.

An online site builder is similar to a website editor except run entirely online instead of through your computer. Site builder services are provided by larger web hosting companies (such as GoDaddy) though often for an extra fee. The online site designer will have a similar interface as a web editor like Dreamweaver or KompoZer. Since you're building your sites directly on the host, though, you don't have to worry about uploading them with an FTP program, and you can use any device to edit your website, not only one computer with the software installed.

Even if you're using site editing software or an online site builder, basic knowledge of at least HTML and CSS will be very helpful in making your site look and feel the way you want. Even if you don't know how to code them, you should understand what they do and be able to interpret them when you see them.

A Content Management System (CMS) is a piece of software you install directly on your web host (not your computer) that streamlines the addition of necessary site features like tags and categories for pages, search and archive functions, or forums and comment sections.

When you use site builders or site editors, each of these features will have to be added manually, which can be incredibly time-consuming even if you are a web coding expert. Content management systems also make it a lot easier to redesign the look of your overall site.

CMS software does take up space on your server and websites run with a CMS use more RAM and CPU than those made by a site editor. On high traffic days, this could mean your pages are slow to load or could cause problems with resource limits if you're using a shared server.

You also don't get quite as much creative control over the features and design elements of the page as you would designing it completely on your own. The main advantage of CMS software is that it lets you focus on the content. You don't have to worry about fixing lines of code or manually adjusting your pages when you decide on a new layout—meaning you have more time to work on the important things.

There are several blogger-specific CMS programs on the internet, many of which you can use for free. WordPress is probably the most common. I know what you're thinking—isn't WordPress one of those free blogging sites? It can be (WordPress offers free blog hosting), but you can also download it as software and install it on your domain.

It's certainly not the only product on the market, though; take your time and carefully consider what features you'll ideally need. Just like with changing domain names, changing CMS software can be a headache and a half if you have to do it down the road.

Blogger success story: Ruhul Amin

Ruhul Amin is the founder of Tips and Tricks HQ, an Australian-based blog aimed at educating other bloggers about WordPress and other technical aspects of blogging. Not only is his site impeccably designed and very successful, but it can also be a valuable resource for new bloggers who aren't so sure on the technical side of things.

Amin stresses the importance of a quality domain name in his posts, and has a few tips for readers: use keywords, make it easy to remember, and keep it short. Amin advises, "It is important for a visitor to get an idea of what the website is about just by looking at the domain name…if [visitors] can't remember the domain name then you run the risk of losing potential traffic."

One more tip from Amin: remember that you can use hyphens between words in domain names if it helps with the overall readability as he does on his site (www.tipsandtricks-hq.com). Not only can this make the name of your blog clearer to visitors, but it can also be a way to get the perfect domain name if the un-hyphenated version was purchased.

Chapter 3: Building your brand

Your brand is the foundation of your blog's identity and purpose. In his article "7 rules of successful bloggers," Robert Pagliarini defines your brand as "the emotional reaction someone feels when he or she hear your name." You have a brand right now, even if you don't realize it—in fact, you probably have several.

You have a certain brand when you're at work, another with your family, perhaps even different ones with various groups of friends. For many new bloggers, that's part of the problem. Your real-life brands are too diverse and scattered to make for a compelling blog; you need to narrow and craft your brand into a salable package.

A brand is a combination of your persona and your reputation. Your persona is the way you try to present yourself to others; your reputation is formed by the way you interact with them. When you're first starting out as a blog and haven't yet built a reputation, you're going to be working off of the strength of your persona alone. It's necessary, then, to decide what your brand will be before you start writing your posts, and then to reinforce that brand consistently through your content.

Play to your audience

Imagine your ideal reader. Think about how they spend their time. Are they single, or do they have a family? Where do they live? What are their values? Tailoring your brand to your audience can help give you a better focus for your first few posts and help you to establish your identity more quickly.

Of course, you shouldn't take this too far, either. Don't pretend to be a new person just to attract more readers. You're not changing your personality, just identifying which aspects of it will be the most appealing to your target reader. Consider it this way: when you're at work, you probably dress differently, have a different bearing, and use a different vocabulary than when you're hanging out with your buddies at the bar or watching TV with the kids at home.

All these versions of yourself are "you," you're just tailoring them to the situation. Most people do this subconsciously in response to the non-verbal cues and clues of their surroundings. With blogging, you can't see the people you're interacting with; without those context clues, it's necessary to construct the persona you want to use rather than letting your subconscious do it for you.

Think about your ideal image. Do you want to be a friendly confidant? A knowledgeable expert? Think back to the "why me?" question you answered in chapter 1. If the reason you chose your niche is because you've studied that topic and have a lot of knowledge to share, your brand might be aimed at educating your readers.

That branding won't work if you're a relative novice in your topic area; maybe instead your brand would be learning how to become a better chef, or finding the best attractions in your city, and bringing the reader along for your discoveries.

If you're having trouble thinking of what you want your brand to be, some old fashioned brainstorming may just do the trick. Get out a blank piece of paper and a pen. Write "I want my blog to be..." large at the top of the paper, then write down whatever words come to mind. Link these words together into concepts and sentences, rearranging and connecting them until you feel like you've gotten to the heart of what you're trying to represent.

You've probably heard the term "elevator pitch," a description of your product or idea that could be conveyed in the time it takes to ride in an elevator—about thirty seconds, if you want to put a number on it. Before you start blogging, you should be able to give an elevator pitch of your brand and topic. Once you can do that, you should have a clear enough concept of your brand to stay consistent through your early posts.

The importance of design

The layout and design of your blog will give your reader their first impression of you. On the practical side of things, you want to make sure it's both easy to navigate and easy to read. Important posts should have a prominent place on the page, and the color scheme shouldn't interfere with the legibility of your writing.

A pre-made template like those available on WordPress can be a good place to start when you're designing your blog, but you should customize at least a few elements of it to help it stand out from the thousands of others that use that same layout. The design you choose for your blog should in some way reflect your brand or niche. Ideally, a reader should be able to glance at your page without reading a word and get a basic idea of your blog topic.

Layout and color choices have some role in this; if you run a photography blog, you should choose a format that emphasizes images, for example. Consider specialized features. A financial blog might find it helpful to install a live tracker of the stock exchange on their front page; a sports blogger might have a ticker of scores and match results.

A great way to clarify your brand is to design a logo that reflects both your niche and your personality. You can do this yourself if you're artistic, but for many people, it's worth the financial investment to hire a freelancer to design the logo for you. The logo will come to represent your brand in most readers' minds, and the initial investment you make hiring a designer will be repaid many times over by the boost to your brand recognition.

Though this is most important with your logo, it can also be true of other aspects of your blog design. If you want customized images or a unique layout format but don't have the design or coding background to make them competently yourself, don't be afraid to look for a freelancer to complete the work for you. A well-designed site will be more likely to attract visitors and will ultimately be worth the initial financial investment.

Blogging success story: Nicola Lees

Nicola Lees had already built a successful career in television before she started TVMole.com. She developed a strong brand based on her expertise, helping people with ideas for TV shows to pitch those shows to TV executives and producers.

The content on TVMole all reinforces this strong brand, giving helpful advice that readers can't get anywhere else, allowing her blog to grow and expand into multiple income streams. She does consult and contract work, speaks on panels and sells books and courses that help her readers.

Having worked with major industry leaders like the BBC and Discovery Chanel meant Lees' obvious choice was to base her brand around her expertise. Her insider perspective makes her a trusted voice in the niche of television production.

But even though she had the credentials, it was still Lees' high-quality and trustworthy content that reinforced her brand on her blog and helped her generate traffic and opportunities.

Chapter 4: Planning and Goals

When someone's getting ready to start a brick-and-mortar small business, he or she are often advised to come up with a business plan before he or she even find funding or look for a location. Because of the amounts of money involved, investors want to know that the owner has thought about every aspect of their business—and most importantly, has planned out how it will make money and grow—before they are willing to back the concept.

While you don't need to hustle for investors when you're starting a blog, a bit of goal-oriented planning is still the best way to make your blog a profitable venture instead of just a hobby and time-sink.

Remember that overnight successes are very rare, not just in blogging but in every area of life. The work you put in at the beginning of the process may not begin to generate returns until a year or more has passed. If you're not ready to play the long game, you're likely to give up too soon and never see your blog reach its full potential.

You won't need to invest much money in starting a blog, but you will need to commit your time consistently enough to be seen as dependable by your readers. Schedule yourself at least an hour to work on your blog every day. Commit to it as much as you would shift at your place of employment. If you don't treat your blog like it's important, you can't expect the readers to feel any differently.

Setting realistic goals

Everybody would love to be making a six-figure income from home talking about one of your passions. That's not an unrealistic goal in the long-term. The problem is that a lot of people think they'll start a blog and within a few months make enough to retire. When they don't achieve this pinnacle of success right away, they get discouraged and give up.

Setting realistic goals doesn't mean you can't dream big. It instead means breaking those big dreams down into pieces and figuring out what short-term steps you can take to achieve long-term success.

First of all, you should determine just what your long term goals are. Where does blogging fit into your ideal future? Is it something you eventually hope to use as your primary source of income or do you see it as simply one part of a larger whole? The amount of effort you'll have to put in to build a blog into a full-time job is very different than what will be required just to make some spending cash on the side.

If you own a small business or product line, a blog may be more your way of communicating with your customers than it is your primary source of income—an integral part of the entire package, but not your main income stream. If you do hope to make blogging your full-time job, you should treat it like a part-time job from the outset; if it's intended as a side project, you can take more time to let it grow.

Once you've thought about your long-term goals, do some research on other blogs in your niche. Start by looking at the most successful and most popular ones. How many page views and comments do most of them get?

How often do they post? How many followers do they have on Facebook and Twitter—and how long has it taken them to get to this point? If the top blog in your niche has 3,000 followers, setting a goal of 5,000 followers in your first six months would most likely only set yourself up to fail. Set smaller milestones. If you want 1,000 subscribers, you first have to get 100 subscribers. Then you can go for 500, and so on, giving you benchmarks of achievement to hit along the way.

Scheduling your posts

There are two levels to consider here, and you should sketch out a plan for both before you start writing your content. There's the week-by-week scheduling of when you want your posts to come out, and there's the monthly and yearly scheduling of points or events you want to hit.

A lot of bloggers just post when the spirit strikes them. They might have four posts in three days and then a two-week gap until the next one. That's fine if you're a hobbyist or if the blog isn't your primary income stream, but to make your blog profitable, it's better to keep a regular schedule on which your readers can depend. Exactly when you post will depend on your niche.

News-based blogs may need to be updated daily to feel current. For less time-sensitive topics, you could choose select days of the week. As always, consider your target audience. A business blog might want to have a post in their subscriber's inboxes every weekday morning; e-mails sent over the weekend would be less likely to be viewed.

A blog about nightlife in the city might want to put out a big post on Thursday when subscribers are making plans for the weekend. Whatever your niche, a weekly schedule lets your readers know when they should expect to hear from you and will more effectively build a strong subscriber base.

The yearly scheduling will be more useful for managing your content and identifying the times interest in your niche will be highest. Some of these things will be universal—any blogger who sells products should make note of the Christmas shopping season on their yearly calendar—but many will be more individual to your niche.

A gardening blog might want to time a new product release to correspond with late winter or early spring when lots of readers will be planning their gardens. A parenting blog could have special content for back to school season. By writing it all out, you can more clearly see what points in the year you want to build toward and where you might have a harder time coming up with content, allowing you to plan accordingly.

Collaboration

Collaboration with another blogger can be an easy way to keep the site running smoothly while at the same time spreading out the pressure and the workload involved in maintaining it. It lets each of you take time off when you need to, and can also help to add more perspectives to the blog's content, expanding its appeal. Just make sure you choose your collaborating partners carefully.

It should be someone you get along with, but also someone you can count on to do their fair share of the work. Ultimately, the goal is for this to be a profitable business venture, and you should make sure from the outset that everyone involved is on the same page and committed to that cause. Even if the person is a family member or close friend, it's a good idea to write up and sign an agreement together just to make sure the expectations are clear.

Blogging success story: Lance Nelson

When Lance Nelson decided to start his blog, he picked an extremely detailed niche. Banskoblog.com is in the Bansko ski resort in Bulgaria. Nelson turned this relatively limited niche into a full-time job that brings in over 60,000 euros per year in income, and his successful branding had a lot to do with the speed and degree of his success.

Everything on his site, from the mountains on his logo to the weather tracker widget and menu options, clearly tells the reader just what he is about, and this precise branding paid off for him in a big way.

Being a skiing blogger means that Nelson has to think very carefully about the scheduling of his content. His readers are going to be most interested during the skiing season, and he has a ready-made audience in the winter; his challenge was how to sustain his readership in the summer months when there's no snow for skiing.

Nelson posts about other topics in the summer that are of interest to his readers. He travels throughout Bulgaria and shares his travels with his readers (who might themselves be looking for something to do during the summer, since they can't ski). Even if you're not in such a weather-dependent niche, thinking about what your ideal readers will be doing throughout the year can help you figure out the right content for the moment.

The Art of Blogging

There are three major factors in a blog's success: The quality of the content, the size of the audience, and how well it's networked into the community. The one of these that you as a blogger have the most control over is the content itself. Though there are things, you can do to increase the size of your readership and make networking contacts if your content isn't up to snuff you won't be able to build a dedicated audience or get backlinks from other blogs no matter how aggressively you advertise your product.

Remember always to think about your audience and pay attention to the trends happening in your niche whenever you're working on your blog, whether that's writing a post or interacting with your readers. Something that works for a political blog might not be as well-suited for a gardening blog, and vice versa. Variety is also important to holding your reader's interest.

If you can, switch up the lengths of posts and the ratio of images to text now and then. A fashion blogger might follow up a long piece on a recent show she attended with a quick blurb about a new purse from her favorite designer. Be as creative and open-minded with the style of your posts as you are with the content.

Chapter 5: Quality content

You've likely heard before that "content is king," and it's true. Quality content is what will build your following and bring opportunities for profit and expansion. You want the posts on your blog to provide value to your reader and to be interesting to read. It should also be professional and free of distracting errors. Readers will usually forgive the errant typo or verb disagreement, but it'll be harder to convince your reader to trust you if you consistently have issues with English mechanics.

The spelling and grammar checker on your word processor will catch most errors; even if you're confident in your writing ability, run it on every post before it goes up to eliminate silly typos and errors. If you know, spelling and grammar are tough for you, get a copy of The Elements of Style by William Strunk and E.B. White. Give it a read then keeps it at the desk where you'll be working, to consult when needed.

The ideal length of a typical blog post is around 300-700 words. It should have a headline that makes the reader want to click on it (though be wary of "click bait" style titles that are intentionally misleading). The content should have a logical flow, with major ideas clearly highlighted in bulleted lists or separated paragraphs.

When you first start your blog, all of the posts you put up should be directly related to your niche. You want to convey your brand from the start, so readers know what to expect from you. You also want to demonstrate your knowledge about the field you're writing in—to establish your expertise with the topic, and show readers why they should care about your opinions.

Your first 10-15 posts should be directly related to your niche. Some very successful bloggers do occasionally go off-topic, but that should wait until you've established your identity.

Core content

Blogging expert Yaro Starak talks about something called a "pillar article" in his advice columns. Chris Garret calls it "flagship content," while Brian Clark calls it "cornerstone content." All of these experts are describing the same basic thing: the articles that give your reader a clear conception of your niche and your opinions about it.

Core content articles should be on the long side—around 500-1,000 words, depending on the format. These posts should not be time dependent; a reader who sees the post a year from now should still find it to be relevant. These posts are the most likely to receive backlinks from other websites and ideally will continue to bring in new readers long after you initially post them.

So they don't get buried in your archives, it's a good idea to list these posts in a separate area, whether that's a drop-down menu or links in a sidebar—this lets new readers easily access the most useful content. You can also reference these articles yourself in future posts to help new readers find and read them.

The more of these core content posts you include on your blog, the better. Five is a good minimum, and you should include at least two in your first ten posts. The ultimate goal of any good core content post is to teach your readers something, whether it's a skill related to your niche, an explanation of a concept, or an opinion piece that will help them see your niche in a new way. If you're not sure what kind of article to write, some core content options are listed below, and might help give you an idea of where to start.

Glossary pages are lists of terms related to your niche that you define for the reader in your own words. Glossary pages are often a useful tool if your niche is related to technology, finance, law, or any other field that has very specific or esoteric terminology. They're also a great format for getting backlinks because other blogs might reference your page if they don't have glossary pages of their own.

Step-by-step how-to articles teach your reader how to do a task or make a product, often with pictures at key steps. Recipe posts on cooking blogs fit into this category and are probably the most familiar example, but this article style applies to almost any niche. Think of something in your industry that you know how to do and your readers might not—the key thing here is sharing your knowledge of something with which you're experienced.

Whitepapers are similar to how-to articles but go into more depth. A whitepaper is typically a 2-10 page document that teaches readers about a concept or topic related to your industry. It should be an all-encompassing solution to a common problem in your niche. Rather than being a single long blog post, it's often best to present whitepapers as PDFs readers can download. You could also type the content into several blog posts and link them together in a series.

List articles are excellent core content because people love to read and share them, and they can be good for stirring up a conversation in your comment section. They can take a few forms. Advice lists give readers tips on how to accomplish tasks ("4 ways to get better sleep" or "5 things to do before you get a mortgage"). Ranked lists are ideal for pop culture or product-based blogs, which can also link to products sold by an affiliate to increase the article's profitability. Informative lists share knowledge with the reader ("most under-rated horror movies" or "surprise benefits of green tea") and can be useful in any niche.

Opinion pieces and editorials are most often seen in political and social commentary blogs, and can be especially useful for stirring up controversy in your comments section. These pieces should start with a clear thesis statement, whether that's a theory, an opinion, or an argument. Back up your argument with well-presented arguments and make sure the thought is unique—remember, you want to add new value to your industry, not rehash the same ideas presented elsewhere. Also, make sure your opinion reinforces your established brand.

SEO

SEO stands for Search Engine Optimization, and how important it is to getting good results in search engines is still up for debate in the blogging community. The idea of SEO is that by using keywords in the course of your posts, you can get higher rankings on results lists when users search for those terms, meaning you'll get more visitors to your site. Nobody debates that this is something that will help you; what blogging experts disagree on is how much you have to focus just on your keyword density.

If you are writing good content that's strongly related to your niche topic, your posts will naturally be very keyword-dense without you putting in any special effort. An over-emphasis on keyword density can make your posts feel repetitive or stilted. Putting way too many keywords in your posts also makes you look like a spammer (called "keyword stuffing") and makes search engine spiders ignore you if you're guilty of it.

The most important places to emphasize keywords in your posts are in the page header and the title tag. When you're naming your pages, make them search engine in a friendly way by giving them names that clearly express what the page is about rather than an in-house classification system. Keep the content itself focused on the idea and don't worry so much about getting terms shoved in there—if it's on the topic to your niche, it will come up in search results naturally. A better way to optimize your search engine ranking is to link back to your own pages periodically.

The more links a page has to it, the more likely it is to show up higher on the search result list. Just like with the keywords, don't over-do it. Reference past posts when it's logical to do so, not just for the sake of SEO.

Finding your voice

Many people make the mistake of wanting to present a perfect image of themselves to their readers. While you do want to present yourself as someone the reader can trust, you also want to show them that you're a real person. There are thousands of blogs out there about every topic imaginable, and ultimately your personality and opinions are what will make your blog the one readers want to read.

Be willing to share your failures, challenges, and struggles. It will make you more relatable, and the reader will ultimately trust you more if they know you're the kind of person who can admit to your mistakes.

A good blog post should have the tone of a conversation between friends. If you're not sure just how to do this, there are a couple of tricks you could try. Try imagining that you're talking to a person in your life, like a sibling or a friend, when you write your posts. How would you explain concepts in your field so that your sister can understand them? Use the same language when you're writing that you'd use out loud in friendly conversation.

Especially if you're not a trained writer, terms like "voice" and "tone" can sometimes be hard to wrap your head around. What does a "friendly tone" mean? Imagine yourself again speaking to that same friend about the topic you're covering in your post, but instead of going straight to your keyboard, record yourself answering the question out loud. Listen to the recording.

Transcribe the sentences you're especially fond of, then fill in around those lines trying to match that tone. Once you've written the post, read it out loud again, then go back and change the places that feel awkward or too formal. As you get more comfortable with the writing process, you'll be able to get that conversational tone straight on the page.

Consistency and trust

One of the most important things is to build the reader's trust. Make sure your content is always factual and original. If you make a habit of parroting or even outright copying someone else, your blog is adding no new value to your reader's life. Your opinions should be yours, and you should be prepared to stand by them. If your readers feel like you're reliable, they'll be more likely to give you their loyal readership.

You can also be dependable for your reader by posting on a regular schedule and not missing posts when you can help it. Some bloggers post daily; others post on select days of the week. Twice a week is a good frequency when you're just starting out. You're posting often enough to give people a reason to keep coming back, but you still have time for the other aspects of your blog, like finding advertisers and communicating with your readers, without making you feel overwhelmed.

Blogging success story: Hero Brown

Hero Brown is the founder of MuddyStilettos.co.uk, "The Urban Guide to the Countryside" for rural areas in England. Brown started the blog as a hobby in 2011 when she moved to rural Buckinghamshire and couldn't find any good information on the area. By 2013, it had become her full-time job, with 5,000 subscribers, 6,500 followers on Facebook and Twitter, and 15,000 unique readers every month.

Brown's background was in magazine editing, and she brings that into her personal style on the site. In an interview with Forbes contributor Hester Lacey, Brown said of her blog, "I think of Muddy Stilettos as an online magazine. It's well-researched, well-written and I'm constantly thinking about my readers. Lots of blogs by their nature are a kind of stream of consciousness. I came at it more from an editorial angle."

Brown is also very dedicated to being trustworthy for her readers, especially in whom she chooses to have as advertisers on her site. "I could earn more money from advertising if I was less fussy," Brown says later in that interview, "but if I don't keep that high-quality bar, the whole reason for reading Muddy Stilettos disappears." By thinking about her audience and keeping their needs in mind, Brown has made a very successful product with Muddy Stilettos that only continues to grow.

Chapter 6: Growing your readership

Having an established readership is the best way to attract attention from advertisers. The broader your audience, the more likely you will be to get ad clicks or to sell products that either you or your affiliates have up for sale on their site.

The exact size of your target audience will likely depend a lot on your niche. Blogs in more specialized niches will tend to have a smaller but more dedicated following than those in fields that generate a lot of popular interest.

In truth, while the niche you've chosen can help you to guess what your target audience might look like, you won't really know your readership until you have them. Most blogging interfaces will give you fairly detailed statistics on how often your pages are viewed, and how many of those page views are "unique" (meaning visits from a different guest) or how many are repeat visits. Check on these statistics periodically.

What style of the post seems to get the most views? Do your readers like posts that are image-heavy or text heavy? How long are your most-viewed posts? Using this information can help you to refine future content, tailoring it to what your audience wants. The more value your reader gets from your posts, the more likely they'll be to link to them and share them with other people, and the better chance you have of increasing your subscriber base.

Have a conversation with your readers

We talked about a conversational tone in chapter 5, and that's certainly important, but it's equally crucial to engage your readers in actual conversation. Always respond to any comments left on your blog posts, so your readers know that you're listening and interested in what they have to say.

You can also engage them in conversation on other social media formats. Set up Twitter and Facebook pages for your blog that are separate from any personal social media accounts you have. Make sure you're as active on those accounts as you are on your blog page, and just like with blog comments, make sure to respond to any Tweets or Facebook comments from your followers just like you would on the blog.

Posting regularly and replying to comments helps cement that view in readers' minds of you as being someone they can rely on and want to spend their time reading. One-off visitors can be useful, but cultivating a base of loyal readers is the best way to increase your subscription and page view numbers, and ultimately the best way to increase your profits.

Interactive content can also help engage your readers. The easiest way to do this is to post polls or surveys occasionally as part of your posts. If you run a fashion blog and post about the best-dressed celebrities on the red carpet at an awards show, you can ask the readers who they thought was the best dressed after you post your opinions.

These can be fun ways to start the conversation and include the readers in your process. If you have the chance to do an interview with someone in your field, you could invite the readers to post questions. Giveaways and contests are also a great way to involve your readership and build the loyalty up into a community.

Entice subscribers

When it comes to readership groups, your subscribers are far more important than your Twitter followers or your Facebook likes. That is your core group of readers who will hear from you directly When you create a post or send out an e-mail blast, and the people who are going to be most likely to spend their money on your products, and the group you can count on for views of your most recent posts. Especially when you're first starting out, growing your subscriber list should be one of your top priorities.

One easy way to increase your subscribers is to offer an incentive to people who sign up. Blogging professionals call this "improving your value" in a potential subscriber's eyes; cynics would call this "bribing people." Whatever you call it, it's a proven, effective way to increase subscriptions. The key is to offer an incentive that gives real value to subscribers without cutting into your profit margin.

An exclusive whitepaper or resource can make a great sign-up incentive because it's something you only have to create once that still gives readers long-term value. If you sell products or services on your site, you could offer a discount to subscribers, either as a one-time coupon or a lower "subscriber rate." Discounts can build both customer loyalty and your bottom line. Someone who wouldn't have looked at your store before might do so if he's got a coupon.

Make it easy for people to subscribe to your site. Pop-up subscription invitations are the current trend. Some readers will find them annoying, and some ad blocking software will prevent them from opening, but they also can be effective at letting readers know you have a mailing list. If you'd rather put a link on your site, make sure it's easy to find and clearly visible to most visitors—don't hide it in a menu or at the bottom of the page. A new visitor shouldn't have to search for a way to get updates when you post.

Blogging success story: Alborz Fallah

Alborz Fallah started his blog CarAdvice.com.au as a side project while he was still working a full-time job. His is an excellent story to show that someone can start a new blog in an oversaturated market (like car review sites) and still manage to be successful by carefully focusing on your target audience.

Rather than trying to compete with every car blog in the world, Fallah focused in on blogging about cars for fellow Australians. His blog generated massive traffic, enough that he got investors interested in his product and has since quit his day job to focus on the blog full time.

Fallah started in 2006 as a one-man team on a site making $10 per day on AdSense. CarAdvice now has a 30-man team of experts with test garages and offices in Sydney, Melbourne, Brisbane, and Perth. The site receives over 300,000 unique monthly visitors and makes over $3 million per year in revenue—all because Fallah understood that he had to target the right audience to be successful.

Chapter 7: Networking and community

Even if you write in a relatively limited niche, chances are there will be at least a few other bloggers out there writing about your topic. In a broad sense, this is your niche's community. The more popular the topic, the larger the community it will be, and the smaller sub-communities will exist within the main. In some ways, you can imagine the blogosphere like a high school, where people talk mostly to the people in their clique—and just like in high school, all the cool kids tend to hang out together.

There are three ways you can approach the existence of the community. You can ignore them and not concern yourself with what others are writing. You can take a passive interest, following them to keep up with what they're saying but not interacting with their site.

Or you can actively engage with them, leaving comments on their posts or linking back to them in your own. You don't have to engage with other bloggers to be successful, but being active in the community is one way to help grow your readership more quickly.

You also don't have to limit yourself to interacting with bloggers in your field. Become an active reader and follower of any blogs you enjoy, even if they're not necessarily related to your own. At the very least, other readers who find your comments to be insightful might check out your blog and find it interesting.

Making friends with other bloggers and website owners can help you generate more traffic by getting your name out in more places. The more a blog post is linked to and visited, the more it will show up in Google searches, which in turn will bring you even more traffic.

Remember that whenever you're posting a comment on someone else's blog, the comment should be primarily about them, and very minimally (or not at all) about you. Link back to your own blog only if it's legitimately relevant to the topic of the post. Spamming people's comment sections with advertisements for your blog will not make you any friends, and will not land you as many readers in the long-term as if you become known for leaving witty, insightful, or helpful comments.

You might feel anonymous when you're interacting with people on the internet, but you should also remember that it's a place where reputation is everything and information can spread very far, very quickly. Be as kind, courteous, and polite in your online interactions as you would be with people face to face. Remember that everything you do online related to your blog is a reflection of your brand. A spirited debate in a comment section can get attention from potential readers, but always be respectful of other bloggers, even when you disagree.

Face to face networking

One of the bizarre things about blogging as a profession is that even if your posts reach 10,000 people every day, it's possible you'll never physically interact with any of them. Attending networking events and conferences can remind you that there are faces and people behind each post and comment.

There are seminars and workshops aimed at bloggers. These can certainly be helpful in that you can meet other bloggers and learn from their experiences, but they're not the best place to meet your followers, too. Attending events or conferences related to your niche can provide excellent networking opportunities both with other bloggers and your potential readership. If you blog about movies, attend a local comic con.

For bloggers in tech fields, trade shows can be great places to see the latest innovations and meet fellow enthusiasts. You can pretty much guarantee some of the other attendees will be bloggers in your field, and even on the off chance you don't make any networking connections, you'll learn something from the event to share with your readers.

Blogger success story: Michael Dunlop

The creator of IncomeDiary.com has been making money on the internet from the time he was a teenager and at 21 has already become a prominent figure in the blogging world. In an article on his site entitled "The True Story of my Overnight Success," Dunlop talks about a web design website he ran before starting Income Diary, called ShoutGFX. He got the idea for the site from another popular design website and thought he could profit from a similar model. He took several members of the original forum with him to his new site.

ShoutGFX ultimately was brought down when members did the same thing, starting their own business based on Dunlop's concept. Though his business also suffered from bad coding (a demonstration of another point: when it comes to outsourcing work, you often get what you pay for), the ultimate lesson Dunlop took away was that "what goes around comes around." Kindness repays the kindness, but if you're underhanded, you'll attract others of a like mind.

Dunlop goes on in the article to talk about one of the biggest keys to his success: seeing his failures as learning experiences rather than crushing defeats. If you want to grow your brand, you occasionally will have to take risks and experiment with new things. Some of them will work out; some of them won't. If you learn from it, though, no experience is ever wasted. Rather than give up when he faced setbacks, Dunlop continued to push forward and now earns a six-figure income as a full-time blogger.

Maximizing Profit

There are three main ways that bloggers make money: advertising income (money advertisers pay you for space on your site), affiliate income (commission received from another company when they sell a product through your site), or a direct sale (reader payment to you for a product or service offered on your site).

Advertising and affiliate income are passive income sources. This is not to say you have no control over the income; you can use page positioning and content to maximize viewer clicks, and can control which advertisers operate on your page, but you are not directly responsible for the product. These are the easiest and most common sources of income for bloggers, but require you to get a large amount of traffic to generate legitimate income.

Direct sales can take a lot of different forms. In a direct sale, you are responsible for delivering a product to the reader. Direct sales can be something that you make and ship to them, an eBook or PDF that's sent to their inbox as soon as they purchase it, or a membership to a forum or directory that members pay for on a monthly or yearly basis.

A graphic designer or photographer might use their blog in conjunction with a freelancing business, using the blog as a platform to gain new clients. It could also be your services as an industry expert and blogger that are up for sale. Paid speaking engagements, consultations, or classes and workshops are all income streams under the direct sale umbrella that many successful bloggers use to increase their earnings.

Chapter 8: Advertising

Most people who set out wanting to write a blog to make money—rather than those who start as hobbyists and grow into businesses—do so imagining they'll make all their money through advertising. Just write a few posts, toss some banner ads on there, and you've got yourself a cash cow. Right?

Well, not quite. The major thing you need to make money from advertising is a lot of traffic, and for a fledgling blog with just a handful of page views per day, you're not going to find too many people who want to pay you money for space on your site. A good rule of thumb is to get at least 10,000 page views per month (that's between 300 and 400 views a day) before you go out looking for advertisers.

Larger ad networks and companies may want sites to show 20,000 or even 100,000 views per month before they'll be interested in securing advertising space. While the exact numbers advertisers are looking for will depend on your niche, 10,000 views a month is a good baseline goal to set for yourself if you'd like advertising to serve as one of your revenue streams.

Google AdSense

The largest ad network for blogs and other websites currently on the internet is Google AdSense. It's the one that many new bloggers turn to because it has an open acceptance policy in regards to different niches and traffic levels. A slower blog will make less money than a high-traffic site, of course, and there are some ad formats that are only available to people with higher viewership counts.

AdSense is easy to use compared to most ad networks. The flip side of this ease, of course, is that Google takes a cut of the advertiser's money as a commission for providing the ad service—about 32% of what the advertiser pays per click goes straight to Google.

The exact amount that you can make using Google AdSense varies depending on what size and style of ad you use, what niche your blog is in, and how much traffic you get. There are three different bid models that advertisers can use to pay for the space on your page. The cost-per-click model is the most common. In this model, you get a commission every time a visitor clicks on the ad, even if they don't go any further through the site.

There's also a cost per thousand impressions model, where you get paid per thousand ad views, even if the viewers don't engage with the ad. The third type is the cost per engagement model, where the advertiser pays you for each time a viewer completes a specified task, like watching a video or completing a survey.

Knowing all of this is valuable in gaining more insight into how AdSense works, but one disadvantage of using AdSense over more selective ad networks is that you don't get to control which kind of ad goes on your page. Google determines which one will work best given your niche and your traffic levels.

Since they're working on commission, they have a pretty good incentive to pick the style and content that's going to make you the most money, but ultimately it's up to Google who advertises on your site and using what format. You control the size and placement of the ad, but that's about it.

Because it's so easy to use (and generates a lot of income in the right circumstances) Google AdSense is often the way to go if you have around 10,000 page views per month and are just starting to work with advertising as an income stream.

Other advertising networks

There are a plethora of different ad networks available for bloggers, most of which will ask for a higher minimum traffic than Google AdSense. Some are highly selective (Revcontent is known for being hard to join and rejects 98% of applicants). There are some that don't require a minimum traffic number to use, making them most useful for new bloggers.

Among these are BidVertiser, Clicksor, and BlogAds. Do some research before signing up with a new ad network. Check out sites that use it to see how it shows up on their pages, and if you can talk to other bloggers about their experience with the site, that's even better.

Keep in mind that the more exclusive ad networks have limited access for a reason. Their advertisers are likely to pay more money in exchange for a guarantee of higher viewership. As your traffic grows, considering larger ad networks could be a good way to increase your profit.

Direct advertisers

Ad networks run on a middle-man profit model. They do the work of finding advertisers and arranging payment, and in exchange, they take a percentage of the money for themselves. Communicating directly with an advertiser means you get to keep all of the money, but it also means you have to deal directly with the companies and negotiate rates and terms.

Direct advertisers are typically a late-stage addition to a blogger's income streams because most direct advertisers will want to see higher traffic numbers than ad networks before committing. It also requires you to be a bit more business savvy than signing up for an ad network.

One situation in which direct advertising could work for a lower traffic blog is if you run a site aimed at a town or community. A small business owner might find it worth his while to advertise on a blog that only gets 5,000 page views per month if all 5,000 of those views are likely to be from potential customers. While direct ads tend to be employed by established blogs, don't rule the idea out if a potential opportunity comes along.

Affiliate income

Affiliate income is when you earn a commission by promoting someone else's products on your site. It's similar to advertising in that it's a passive income stream, and you don't have to produce goods or services, but unlike advertising, you only get the income if your affiliate makes a sale. Though high-traffic websites are more likely to earn money through an affiliate program, affiliate income can be more profitable for a blog as it's building traffic than advertising income because it doesn't rely strictly on site-view numbers.

Amazon's affiliate program is the best-known and is likely the best place to start. It's easy to sign up for, and the site has such a vast array of products for sale that you're very likely to find something that relates to your niche. Though you can treat affiliate links like advertising and make them a passive element of your page, affiliate products are more likely to sell if you review them or promote them with an actual post.

Though you don't get to control who advertises on your site through an ad network, you do get to control which products you promote through an affiliate program. You should only endorse products that you believe will be useful to your readers if you want to maintain their trust and loyalty. You should also make sure that the product connects logically to your chosen niche.

Improving your ad revenue

As simple as it might sound, where you place the ads on a page can impact your readers' level of engagement with it and subsequently with how much money you can make from it. While banner ads at the top of the page are one of the more common advertising styles, this isn't necessarily the best place to position the ad to get reader interaction. Including the ad within the main space of your posts will increase your average clicks per visit.

While you may not know the companies that advertise on your site when you're using an ad network, if you sign up advertisers directly you should support them whenever possible. This doesn't necessarily mean writing "advertorials" (posts specifically dedicated to promoting advertisers) unless doing so would feel natural and organic to your blog, but you can engage with them in other ways without diminishing the integrity of your site.

Tweet to your advertisers from time to time. Know what they're up to and if they're releasing a new product or have an upcoming event that your readers would benefit from knowing about, be sure to share that information. Anything you can do to increase your value from the advertiser's perspective will only help you to bring in more revenue.

Blogger success story: Daniel Scocco

Daniel Scocco is best-known for running the site DailyBlogTips.com. At this point, Scocco is more focused on his software company and his online marketing training course, rather than overseeing the day to day workings of his blog. Though he does some of the writing himself, he also employs a staff of paid writers and brings other bloggers in for guest posts.

He's grown his blog to the point that it generates a large amount of passive income for him, letting him focus on his other income streams. In a recent year, Scocco was able to make around $100,000 from Google AdSense alone, proving it's possible to make a living wage using AdSense—if you're willing to put in the work to build the site.

Chapter 9: Diversifying your income

As was said in the opening section, blogging is very rarely a stand-alone business. Even if it starts out that way, most bloggers find they can build their revenue more quickly by diversifying their income streams than if they worked off of advertising and affiliate income from their blog alone. Manage your expansions carefully.

Experimentation is the only way to grow your business, but do some pre-planning to make sure you'll be able to maintain the same quality on both your blog and in your new venture before you commit to it. In some cases, you might find it ultimately more valuable to outsource some of the work or bring on a paid writer or assistant to make sure that you're able to juggle all the aspects of your business.

Any new revenue stream you add to your blog should complement it. Remember that good work leads to good opportunities and that reputation is invaluable to your long-term success. It may serve you better to do two things exceptionally than five things that are only of mediocre quality.

Especially if you're going into the realm of product sales, delivering a low-quality product, taking a long time to ship items, or having poor customer service can end up driving readers away instead of helping to reinforce your brand. Strike a balance: you should be willing to experiment and take risks, but should still take the time to think through and plan new ventures, so they have the best chance to be successful.

Your business will change as it grows and progresses. Things that worked well for you when you were first starting out might have less of an impact on your bottom line as you grow;

potential income sources that are ineffective or too risky in an early stage of your blog may become possible after you've developed a following. Again, balance is key. Find the things that work for you and continue to do them, but never stop looking for things that might work better.

Potential income streams

The possibilities for monetizing your blog are truly endless, and while some techniques have proven effective for others, no list of income streams can be truly comprehensive. Don't rule something out just because you don't see anyone else talking about it, but if you're looking for ways to expand your profits from your blogs, consider one of the following options.

Member sites

A paid section of your site can be an excellent way to provide more value to your readers while expanding your income streams, and may be useful for a blog in a smaller niche, whose readership is of the small, dedicated variety. The caveat to this is that you want to make sure that a paid member site is truly providing a significant increase in value over your free content, or you'll risk leaving your most dedicated readers feeling ripped off.

There are many kinds of member-only sites. Forums and directories are popular formats. Carol Tice (who writes the blog Make a Living Writing) added a paid section to her site called The Writer's Den that offers one-on-one coaching and other services for aspiring freelancers, like a job board and boot camps. Since her site helps freelancers make a living, it was a logical and organic extension of her brand.

While a member's only site doesn't require you to make any physical products, it will also require more complex coding than your typical blog page. Unless you've got a background in programming or development, you may need to hire someone to help you set it up. Make sure to plan enough time and money to outsource these projects when you're considering whether or not to try them.

EBooks

The most successful eBooks come from bloggers whose brand is based on expertise. You can either release the eBook as a PDF directly from your site or through a retailer like Amazon for almost no financial investment. It is a time investment to release an eBook. You want to make sure it contains new material that's not just a re-hash of the information readers can get on your blog for free. An effective eBook topic might be an in-depth analysis of a trend in your field or a comprehensive how-to solution of a common problem.

Income from an eBook tends to reach its highest levels shortly after its initial release. Referencing the book in your future posts or running a promotion could cause spikes in sales, but if you're marketing the book, right the bulk of your subscribers will buy it right off the bat if they're going to. Subsequent spikes in sales tend to be from new readers who have come to you since the initial release.

Online courses

Online courses can take many forms for a blogger. The easiest way to make a course is to write it as a series of PDF documents that your reader purchases and studies on their own—very much like an eBook, but with exercises and extra resources designed specifically to educate the reader.

Recording media to accompany the course can make it feel more personal and gives the course more value. Whether you do it as an audio file or a video, people who buy the class will benefit from hearing you explain the concepts out loud. Video can be especially helpful for physical or visual niches, like fitness or design, where demonstrating the concept can be easier than explaining it.

The most time-intensive course style is to meet with the students in real time through a chat room or online education portal. Real-time courses may be the best format for more advanced concepts, where the readers might have a lot of questions that are hard to answer in a book, or for workshop-style courses, designed to help the readers learned from each other as well as from you. The disadvantage of this style of class is that it requires people to be available at a specific time to attend, which may limit interest and attendance.

Workshops and seminars

The same material that you teach in an online course can be put to use in an in-person workshop or seminar. You could present this at an industry conference or set up an independent seminar in your area. The benefit of an in-person lecture or seminar is that it allows your followers to meet and interact with you, which will increase their feeling of loyalty. The disadvantage of seminars is that they can be costly to put on, especially compared to the ease and efficiency of an online course.

Blogging success story: Darren Rowse

Darren Rowse is the founder and editor of ProBlogger Blog Tips and Digital Photography School. Not only has he had great success of his own, but his blog is also one of the best resources on the internet for other bloggers looking for advice. In a 2013 post on ProBlogger, Rowse talked about the 12 distinct income streams he has developed. His blog started as a hobby but got popular enough he experimented with AdSense and the Amazon Affiliate Program after the first year.

Starting from those humble origins, he expanded his brand to include speaking engagements, books, and a consulting service. ProBlogger now features a job board and a member site, both of which contribute steady revenue.

This expansion of his brand took place over the course of a decade. Rowse took risks and wasn't afraid to take on new projects, but also managed his expansion carefully. During the article on his revenue streams posted on ProBlogger, Rowse says, "The key is to pick something to try and see whether it connects with your readership and to learn as much as you can while you're doing it." It's worth noting he no longer offers the consulting service.

Being willing to remove income streams that aren't producing can be as important as adding new ones that are.

Chapter 10: Marketing your blog

You don't need a massive advertising budget to raise your blog's traffic upwards of 10,000 views a month and to get recognized within your niche. We already talked about a few ways to build readership back in chapter 6, but how can you entice even more people to your page?

Facebook and Twitter are certainly good places to start. Don't limit your marketing to asking your friends and family to like your business site. Facebook ads are very inexpensive and can be targeted to ideal readers or groups. Follow other bloggers in your niche on Twitter.

You may get a follow back, and even if not, they could have interesting things to say. It's advice that bears repeating: joining the conversation in your community is one of the best ways you can let people know you exist.

Team up with small businesses

In chapter 8, I mentioned getting direct ad revenue from small businesses, but you can also form more symbiotic relationships with small businesses to help both of you expand your brands. Writing reviews of their products that are then shared on their site will bring more links and traffic back to you at the same time it helps them to sell their products.

Remember that most small business owners are just like you— they're trying to get as much exposure as possible without having to spend a ton of extra money.

Sponsor or host events

If you run a blog about biking, you could become a sponsor for a local bike race. If you run a blog about pop culture, you could host an Oscar viewing party at a local bar or restaurant and live Tweet or chat with your followers.

We tend not to think about in-person events as being useful for a blogger because our target audience is online and can come from any corner of the globe, but don't forget that your area is full of potential readers, even if your niche isn't specifically devoted to your town.

Contests

Saveur.com honors the best foodie blogs in various categories at the end of every year. WriteToDone.com ranks the top blogs for writers. For every niche, there is someone out there ready to recognize the bloggers in the field. Winning an award can be a great way to gain exposure. Some you can enter or get nominated for, and others are based on reader votes, so check out what's going on in your niche and consider how you can put yourself in a good place to compete.

Be charitable

It feels good to give back—and from a branding perspective, it's a great reputation boost and a chance to gain visibility while doing something good. Charity doesn't have to mean giving money to someone, either—in fact, the best opportunities involve donating your time or blog space to a cause.

A fitness blogger might ask readers to sponsor them in a cancer walk, for example, while a financial blogger might put on a series of free workshops for people in a local library or community center to help them better maintain their financial health. Giving back to your readers and the community can establish your name and your brand in the minds of new potential fans.

Blogging success story: John Resig

John Resig found TheChive.com with his brother Leo in 2008. Described by Bloomberg Business as "a crowdsourced, Internet version of a lad magazine—the Maxim of the 21st century," by 2013 The Chive had grown into a massively popular website with 20.1 million unique visitors per month. Though it might seem strange for a site based on funny pictures and cute girls, the Chive owes a lot of its growth and success to its various charitable projects.

Chive readers have raised hundreds of thousands of dollars through Chive Charities that has gone to wounded veterans and sick or underprivileged children around the country. As Resig said in his interview with Bloomberg Business, the site "moved from a website to a brand to culture", one that's a bizarre but successful balance of frat house atmosphere and random acts of kindness.

How has The Chive managed to grow such a successful brand so quickly? They focused on building their audience rather than their profit margin and then capitalized on their loyal fan base by selling branded products and hosting meet-ups across the country.

One user said of the site, "If I see someone in a Chive T-shirt, I know what kind of person they are and that I'll probably get along with them." If you can cultivate that kind of reaction from your fan base, you can consider your blog very successful indeed.

Bonus

Here is your amazing bonus to help you starting out your blog.

You can also read about how to start a blog using The Entrepreneurial Method.

In addition, I have written a blog about the best and quickest 3 ways to earn your first $1,000 in 30 days. Let me know what you think in a comment there.

Also, if you have any questions about the book or the blog, let's have a quick call FREE, I will be glad to help.

My other books that will definitely interest you

The New Rich

New Social Media Platforms in 2016

Thank You

If you enjoy the book and bonus, please leave an Amazon review, it takes only 9 seconds :)

Khalid Zidan